T0197366

# The Spirit of the Tree
## of the Tree
## and Other Backyard Tales

*Connecting to Creation*

*Nancy Nason Guss*

*AuthorHouse™*
*1663 Liberty Drive*
*Bloomington, IN 47403*
*www.authorhouse.com*
*Phone: 1 (800) 839-8640*

*Published by AuthorHouse    11/14/2018*

*ISBN: 978-1-5462-0372-8 (sc)*
*ISBN: 978-1-5462-0374-2 (hc)*
*ISBN: 978-1-5462-0373-5 (e)*

*Library of Congress Control Number: 2017912332*

*Print information available on the last page.*

*This book is printed on acid-free paper.*

*Stories, Illustrations, and Photography by Nancy Nason Guss*

author**HOUSE**®

*To all seeking spiritual peace, joy, and love. May you find a place of solitude where you connect to the beauty and brilliance in the miracles of God's creation.*

"If I ever go looking for my heart's desire again, I won't look any further than my own backyard. Because if it isn't there, I never really lost it to begin with."

-L. Frank Baum, *The Wonderful Wizard of Oz*

# Contents

# Acknowledgments

I am so grateful for this year of reflection and renewal that has brought me peace, joy, and love through daily connection to God in nature. Sometimes this is in my backyard; other times during travels as I listen to the ocean or stare in amazement of incredible sunsets and sunrises over mountains, forests, and seas.

First and foremost, I thank God every day for the magnificent creation of our Earth and all its inhabitants. Just seeing how every little detail, each with its own purpose, works together to create this exciting journey we call life on an amazing planet we call Earth. Thank you, God, for the miracle of life and letting me share in it for this short time.

I would like to thank my husband, Bernard Guss, who shares a love of our backyard garden and nature walks. He has been my nurturer in this journey, my amazing life partner, as well as my helper in tending our garden.

I would like to thank my parents, George Nason and Patricia Woodward Nason (deceased) for sharing the love of God that has provided me strength, love, and guidance throughout my life.

A special thank you goes to my grandmother, Elizabeth Riley Woodward, for introducing me to her bird feeder by the window, taking me fishing with a cane pole, and creating her gladiola garden that brought so much beauty and joy for her and us. It is her love for these little pieces of creation that has found a permanent place in my heart and brought joy to my spirit. Thank you, Grams.

Thank you to the neighbors who share our backyards with us, especially Pete, Jane, Stephanie, Kenny, Chance, and Madison. For many years, our shared backyards have been a peaceful place where our children have grown and shared this life journey. I especially want to thank Madison for sharing her time with the tree, rainbow, and me to create some of the final photographs in "The Spirit of the Tree."

Finally, thank you to my amazing and supportive family, extended family, and friends for the gifts of experiences, support, and love. I am blessed.

# Introduction

In the hustle and bustle of life, when the world and its problems spin circles around each person, our heads and bodies are left spinning and spewing in complaint and fatigue. When this happens, people have found a variety of creative ways to deal with this and try to bring peace, but it doesn't always work. Our world's inhabitants seek a variety of escapes, such as, exercise, addictions, or super busyness. In some cases these can work, at least temporarily, but what can a person do to have peace, joy, and harmony that carry them through the toughest journeys of life with contentment, calm, and love?

What is the example we are setting for our children, especially when we are under pressure? They will learn to respond as we do. Are we helping them find ways to bring peace, appreciation of our world, and love to their young lives, even during tumultuous times? This life lesson can be the gift that costs nothing but lasts a lifetime. I am saddened by children suffering from the effects of our virtual world filled with cyberlives, especially when those children lose hope and find nothing to restore the beautiful souls within. If only they could learn at an early age how amazing they and this world are. So, what can we do to create a better world for children and ourselves?

For me, that has been beginning every day with a glass of lemon/lime water, my daily meditation readings, and time on my porch with my backyard garden. Here I sit and share nature with the birds at the feeder, the butterflies, the rabbits, squirrels, and the many forms of wildlife that meet at the little pond behind my house and enact their daily melodies, dramas, and dances.

I pondered on the thought: What if every person could just be at peace for one hour every day in quiet contentment? Then all can experience a moment in joy that costs nothing. Sometimes, we need to forget our wearying world and just reconnect to this creation we have had the privilege to join.

Our wonderful world is here for our enjoyment. May you find such a spot where you can take a moment to enjoy, as have I, the spirit that connects all of us to all the life around us. I hope and pray that you find joy in these little stories that express love of life within the simple pleasure of just being.

> "I come to the garden alone,
> While the dew is still on the roses;
> And the voice I hear, falling on my ear,
> The Son of God discloses.
> And He walks with me, and He talks with me
> And He tells me I am His own
> And the joy we share as we tarry there,
> None other has ever known."
>
> -"In the Garden" by Austin Miles

# The Spirit of the Tree

## Inspired by the aura around our cypress tree

"I think that I shall never see
A poem as lovely as a tree"
-Joyce Kilmer

Cypress tree is one of many in the yard. She may not be the tallest, but she is the fullest, and her shape is the perfect tree shape.

Small birds nest in her branches,
and the herons share perch time at her peak with
the anhingas, kingfishers, and egrets as they
watch the lake below for the fish that will
become their meal.

Butterflies dance gracefully among her branches.

A tiny sparrow sits in the feeder hanging from the lowest branch.

Mama Blue Jay tosses food from the feeder to her babies on the ground. A sentry keeps careful watch from above.

Squirrels playfully chase each other up and down her trunk.

Her beautiful knees provide a haven under the shade for the glossy ibis and moorhens.

Ducks and rabbits eat the seed and rye grass between the cypress knees.

She breathes deeply, and fills her being with carbon dioxide. She exhales the oxygen for the people and animals to breathe. It is the cleanest of air and does not need any filtering or perfumes. It provides the essence of life for so many.

There she stands, tall, mighty, and magnificent.

She is humbled by how lucky she is. She is there together with the other trees to support all forms of life.

In this great big world, one tree helps so many. And when there is more than one tree, even more are helped.

She may not be the one who can run and play, but that is not her job. Her job is to be there and help those around her.

There is a little girl who loves playing outside in her backyard.

She lovingly watches the cardinal family, the mourning doves, mockingbirds, jays, and crows enjoy the beautiful trees. She listens to the chipper chirp of the tiny finches.

She gazes in awe at the creation.

She sees the perfectly shaped tree and feels a special spirit about it. It has a halo of sweet love and comfort.

The little girl places her hand on the tree, feeling the pulse of life and energy. She inhales deeply, filling her lungs with the fresh, clean air that is filled with the oxygen from the tree.

She exhales, and the tree is grateful for the carbon dioxide from the child, with both working together to create clean air for each other to breathe.

As the child gazes up into the branches, she sees the sun beaming down in love for the tree, the girl, and the earth. She hears the music of the birds and feels the warmth of this special and pure love and peace.

The girl marvels at how amazing the creation of the tree is.

The tree marvels at how amazing the creation of the girl is.

They both share a moment marveling at all the life enjoying these same moments together at this little spot in her backyard.

As she gazes into the sky, still holding the tree, she sees the rainbow surrounding her yard with God's promise of love. Her eyes fill with tears of joy in the beauty of this moment.

What she does not know is that at this very moment, many children and grown-ups all over the world are sharing this very same experience at the exact same time. Some are gazing at stars, others at the ocean.

Some marvel from the streets in front of their houses,

and some from high in the mountains.

She realizes that the spirit of life's energy is everywhere. What she does not know is that when every living thing is feeling this love and peace at the same time, only love and peace can exist where they are.

They all become one in love and life and creation.

This is what life really is.
This is where life really is.
This is what keeps life going.
This is what grows the spirit of love.
Now and Forever

The girl says a little prayer:

"Thank you God for this beautiful earth home.
Thank you for the tree and all it does for the animals and me.
Thank you for all life.
Thank you for showing me your miracle that all creation is.
Help me remember this all the time, even when times are hard, or
the world seems mean. The world is not mean here; it is sweet and
good. Thank you for keeping this in my mind, my heart, and my spirit."

As she says this prayer, her eyes light up with gratitude for this special
moment. God answers her prayers with the most beautiful double rainbow
over the tree, her house, and her. All through her life, even when times
are tough, she remembers this blessed moment and feels peace.

As long as she lives, she brings her peace, happiness, and love to all she meets. It is contagious. They feel her spirit of joy whenever she is near. And when she is not there, they remember her joy and share it with others.

The world becomes a better place just like her backyard...

...where the cypress tree grows in love, knowing that this love, when spread, saves the world. From then on, all who see the tree feel peace and joy in the moment. Few know the reason; they just feel it. Occasionally, someone notices the glow of light surrounding this special tree, experiences God's creation, and lifts up a prayer of thanks. The world is a better place, and the magnificence of life's miracles reaches the ends of the earth. Then there is peace. Shalom.

# The Window

Birds' stunning colors
Blue jays, cardinals, parrots
Perfect miracles!

A girl and her grandmother scoop seed from the huge container on the back porch, mix it with apple cores, lettuce scraps, and crumbs, and pour it into the feeder together. They sprinkle more seed on the ground outside the feeder and go back into the house to wait.

The girl gazes out the window at the bird feeder as her grandmother stands behind her to tell her which birds to watch for and to let her know when they arrive. The feeder is just outside the kitchen window, and the girl sits in the chair facing the feeder; the window is the only thing between her and the visiting birds.

As the little one sits in the chair, her grandmother explains, "Be very still, and they will come. If they sense any movement, they will fly away."

The little girl silently sits without moving for what feels like an eternity. Her grandmother sets the table in the dining room as a blue jay flies onto the feeder. The girl remains still, and the blue jay sings his song of thanks for the feast sitting before him.

The blue jay looks up and sees the little girl, and they lock eyes. The girl thinks, "I love him. He is so beautiful." Then she silently tells the blue jay, "Welcome, sweet bird. May you find ample food to nourish you." The blue bird nods in gratitude and pecks at the apple core.

When he has his fill, he glances at the girl, nods a thank you, and flies away.

The little girl walks into the dining room and tells her grandmother about the blue jay. Her grandmother commends her for handling it perfectly. "The birds feel safe and do not fear you when you are quiet and still." The grandmother explains that all animals feel love, and it is important to recognize that each one has a spirit, and all of them have their own natural beauty, just like people. "With animals in the wild, we can't talk to them out loud, but we can communicate our love quietly though our thoughts, and they will sense our peace and love."

The girl spends much of her vacation time in the chair facing the window. She meets many brilliant birds and calls them by their names or titles: Mr. and Madame Cardinal, the red-winged black bird family, Curt the Crow and Gary Grackle, sweet sparrows, Robin Redbreast, Mrs. Quail, and the Mourning Doves of Peace. On occasion, some squirrels disrupt their peace, but she gets to know them, too.

As she grows up, she always has a bird feeder and enjoys the love of God's freest creations. Her grandmother passes away when she is a young adult, and life goes on.

Some years later, she marries and has a daughter of her own,, who is named after the grandmother. Together they watch the feeder by the kitchen window, anticipating the special blue jays, sharing the same love of each of the birds and creatures, and connecting generations past to those yet to come.

# The River Tree's Story

"As I went down to the river to pray
Studying about that good old way
And who should wear
the thorny crown
Good Lord, show me the way."
-Traditional African-
American Spiritual

He is the most unusual tree. Instead of growing straight and tall, he grows sideways, hanging straight over the river. About a quarter of the way across the river, his trunk twists itself, turning straight up to the sky. When the tree loses his leaves in the autumn, people can see his unusual shape. During the summertime, his branches are full, hiding a nest of sweet songbird hatchlings that await their mother. The tree protects the nest, and each leaf surrounding the dear babies brings comfort and safety while their mother searches for food.

Our story begins one summer day as two young brothers carrying cane poles hike the small trail next to the river. They are looking for a place to cast their lines. They finally notice a place where both can sit, so they climb down to the riverbank and stand beside the twist of the tree. They like the shade the tree shares. As they practice casting their lines, they realize that if they cast from that shady site, the hooks will catch the tree above. The tree softly speaks to them saying, **"Not here, you will hurt the baby birds."**

The older brother hears and heeds the message. They look up and see that way up in the tree is the edge of a nest. They smile at how precious it is to see and hear the tiny chirps. The older brother announces, "Let's go farther down so that we do not disturb them." The younger brother marvels at his brother's kind wisdom. As they wander farther, they hear the chirping of the babies and see their mother flying to the nest.

They notice the beautiful shape of the old, unusual tree and admire him from afar. After a moment, the younger boy asks his brother, "Tell me about that tree. You seem to know what he is thinking."

The brother is silent for a moment as he gathers his thoughts. "Two years ago, before you were allowed to wander with me, I found myself at that same spot, where the sun was shining through the trees onto the river. I was tired and just wanted to rest.

"I could see that the twisted tree was like a chair in the woods. I climbed into his seat with my back against the trunk that goes to the sky. I felt comfortable and loved. Then I heard God talking to me. He said. **'Feel the life in the tree. He shares messages with you if you are quiet; listen, and hear him.'** He also told me, **'This is safe and sacred ground where life begins for birds, plants, frogs, and fish in the stream. You must always respect this place.'**

"I looked to the sky and asked God why the tree was so twisted and gnarly, and he told me to ask the tree, which I did.

"I waited for his answer, but instead, I fell into a deep, dreaming sleep. I knew I was safe and secure on his trunk, and so I rested."

The younger brother listens intently to his older brother describe nature's message.

"In my dream, I saw the tree in its youth, growing straight and tall.

Then one day, there was a storm and a big flood. The riverbanks were covered with the rushing river, which crested into large waves over the banks.

"The land around the tree was eroding bit by bit, but his roots hung on the best they could. He helped the land around him stay there, but he was now on his side, hovering perilously above the water. He struggled to hold onto the ground as gravity pulled him closer to the water. His roots, though very young, used all their muscle to hang on. They stretched deeper into the earth to get a solid footing.

"At the end of the storm, he was safe, but not every tree made it. The tree next to him was in the water.

"He decided that he did not want to end up in the water, too, so he held strong for many years. He grew weary from growing sideways, until one special day.

"On that day, he saw the sun peering at him from directly above his head, and he turned his leaves, branches, and trunk in its direction. After time, he was able to straighten part of his trunk, and he grew tall.

"He became less tired as he grew toward the sky. But no matter what he did, he could not straighten out the lower part of his trunk, and this bothered him.

"He asked God why he would not let all of him grow straight and tall, and why part of him remained hovering above the water.

"God told him, **'Things happen in our lives that shape us, and we are to use that shape to help make the world a better place!'"** The brother continues his explanation. "The tree's shape gives a natural place of rest for birds, animals, and people like us. He has a built-in bed that is safe for you and me. He still provides shade, as do all trees, but because his roots are so strong, he generates life from the earth and connects it to God. Do you see how he meets the sky?"

The younger brother looks at the top of the tree into the sky and nods with understanding.

The older boy continues, "We are not to harm him, and he will talk to us. When you sit with him, he shares healing, wisdom, peace, and love."

The brothers remain silent for a moment. The younger brother puts down his pole, walks to the tree, and climbs into the bed, resting in the tree's comfort and safety.

The tree smiles, rustles his leaves, and whispers, "You, my child, are a loved and a beautiful being. I am glad you are here. Rest."

A gentle breeze reassures the boy, and he falls asleep. In his dreams, he hears the tree tell him, **"In your life, you will teach others to love creation and Creator, just as your brother and I are teaching you.**

**Your lesson is to remember that in the storms of life, sink your roots deep, hang on tight, and then let God's light shine on you. When your roots are strong, the storms may change you, but they make you stronger and shape you so that you, too, can help others and bring joy to the world. Your new shape becomes its own beauty.**

**Now, go back to your brother in peace; he is about to catch a fish and will need your help. It will serve you as dinner tonight."**

The boy awakens and walks to his brother, who is holding his cane pole.

When the bobber repeatedly dives up and down, he pulls back and brings a huge fish to the surface. "We will eat well tonight," he proclaims. The younger boy holds the net as his older brother gently removes the fish.

They both express thankfulness to the river, the tree, and the fish for their food, lives, and wisdom. For the rest of their days they honor the river, forest, trees, birds, and all of creation. Most importantly, they grow with strong roots, are shaped by their trials, and use the beauty of their lessons to help provide peace, joy, comfort, and love. They make the world a better place, just as the tree does for them.

"When through the woods and forest glades I wander
And hear the birds sing sweetly in the trees,
When I look down from lofty mountain grandeur,
And hear the brook and feel the gentle breeze.
Then sings my soul, my Savior, God, to Thee;
How great Thou art, how great Thou art!"

-Stuart K. Hine

# The Forgotten Garden

**Miracles do happen.**

After the woman had died, no one was there to notice the tiny desert garden she had on the back porch of her house. No one ventured back there unless it was to put something out that they did not want in the way. The porch grew cluttered, and as the clutter increased, the life slowly ebbed away from the tiny garden.

The tiny garden planter was short and round, hand painted with cactus and birds. As it sat and sat, the painted blue sky faded and chipped off. Each plant slowly died away and dissolved into the soil. The tallest of the group, a Golden Ball Cactus, tried to hang on. She had hoped that someone would find her and just give her some water. The cactus grew tired and weak, so she gave in, shriveled up, and lay down onto the sand.

There she slept for 10 years.

One day, the two daughters of the woman were clearing the back porch. They were saddened by the neglect and mess, so they brought in a large garbage bag and just began cleaning. One bumped against the shelf holding the cactus planter.

The cactus awoke startled and a little disoriented until she saw what was happening around her. She worried when she saw dead plant after dead plant get tossed. Other garden pots, once filled with life, were crumbling in the girls' hands as they picked  them up and tossed them into the large trash bags. Was she going to get tossed, too? "I'm so weak, but I'm still alive," she tried to say. But she could not stand or say anything. All she could do was lie on her side like all the other dead plants.

The older daughter saw the desert garden and planter, picked it up, and gazed at the artwork painted on the sides.

"Mom so loved the desert when she lived there, didn't she?" Her younger sister nodded her head and turned away teary-eyed.

"This was once very pretty. It may clean up okay enough to use again. I think I will take it home and try." She looked at the plants. The little succulents were all withered into shriveled strings on the soil. The cactus was brown and folded on its side across the sand. The daughter noticed something about the cactus and exclaimed, "Look! The very tip of this cactus is still green! There may be a little life left in it! Wouldn't that be amazing after 10 years of neglect! I'm going to try to save it."

So she brought the planter with the cactus into her home onto the back porch, where she did her gardening. She sprayed mists of water onto the cactus.

"Oh my," the cactus thought. "Is it raining?"

The cactus took a long stretch in the cool wonderful feeling of the shower.

The daughter exclaimed, "It is still alive! It's still here! Look! It is straightening right up! This is amazing! It's a miracle!"

With glee, she showed her husband. Her husband was so happy that he went and showed the neighbors! They all cheered, and the cactus felt such a renewal of joy.

It was still thin and brown, but all it needed was a little love and care, and it would be fine!

She lovingly petted the cactus and promised to take care of it.

The cactus loved the sweet attention, and although she was still quite weak, she felt content. She was sorry the other plants around her did not survive, but she could still feel their spirits.

The daughter knew the cactus needed nutrients, water, and light, so she gently dug around the roots and put her on a bench in the sun.

She cleaned the planter and refilled it with fresh soil and sand. She replanted the cactus and added some gravel. The cactus tried standing as tall as she could; still, she was a bit bent. The daughter sensed that the cactus felt a little wobbly, so she gave it a stake for support. To make things even better, she planted new succulents to keep the cactus company and renew the sweet garden. She added nutrients to the soil.

The daughter thought about life, death, and resurrection. The garden reminded her that sometimes things that were thought to be dead still might have life and purpose. They may just need a little nurturing, nutrition, light, fresh soil, and water.

She knew that this was a message from her mother. It lifted her spirits and filled her with hope. She had been quite sad the many years after her mother's passing, and this little desert garden taught her that love and life do not end, and her mother's spirit is still with her.

As the cactus healed, she stood independently and grew strong. Her brown eventually turned to green, and the garden thrived. She grew tall and continues to grow greener and taller to this day.

# The Lady Lily and Curt the Crow

Inspired by these two birds interacting in our backyard.
It was so awesome that I just had to take their picture.

All things bright and beautiful,
All creatures great and small,
All things wise and wonderful,
The Lord God made them all.

-Cecil Frances Alexander

One morning, as Lady Lily Egret walks through the backyard, all the people in the nearby houses turn their heads to admire her grace and beauty. She is a tall, statuesque, magnificent, and majestic bird.

From across the field, Curt the Crow sees food in the shadows near the Lady Lily, and he swoops down to feast on the bounty.

Lady Lily welcomes him, but the people in the houses all comment on how the fat, ugly, scruffy black bird is taking all the seed for himself. One even declares, "I took down my bird feeder because I seemed to get only crows, grackles, and blackbirds. They are nasty."

Curt and Lady Lily both hear these harsh words. Although Curt tries staying calm in spite of feeling very hurt, he cannot let it go. "Caw! Caw!"

Curt cries as he launches himself madly toward the patio and people. He acts like he was going to bite them, but at the last moment, he swoops up and lands on the roof of the porch. "Caw! Caw!"

Lady Lily looks with compassion on her angry and hurting friend. Curt's pride will have none of that, and he lashes out at Lady Lily. "What are you staring at? You probably think I am ugly and nasty, too." He turns his back to her and paces back and forth across the roof.

"No, dear Curt, I do not think that at all. I feel bad for you. Those people judged you by the type of bird you are. That does not seem fair, and I am sorry."

Curt lowers his head, "Thank you, Lady Lily. I am sorry I snapped at you. I was just angry. I seem to do that whenever my feelings get hurt. I tend to take it out on those who happen to be nearby."

Lady Lily smiles and shares her insight. "That anger and hurt you feel is real. I know you wanted to get to those people in the house, but when they saw you swooping at them, cawing fiercely, it made them hold onto their opinions of you being ugly and nasty." Lady Lily pauses to let Curt digest her words.

She continues as Curt listens. "It did not change them at all. An angry face is not one anyone sees as someone they want to be around. You may have better luck with smiling and kindness, and then calmly fly away when they say things."

She walks as close to the house as she dares. "Don't let them know it gets to you, and don't let it get to you. They don't know you. Hold your head high. You know who you are. Don't let them define you."

Curt launches himself off the roof and flies to the palm tree to get closer to Lady Lily and still remain somewhat hidden. It also gives him a moment to think about her words. "That's hard to do!" he replies. "You know, Lady Lily, I get tired of people thinking that some birds are better than others just because our customs and looks are different.

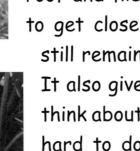

It's frustrating being on the other end, and I can't seem to get them to change their minds. I try visiting often; I bathe in the birdbath, and I stand as tall as I can."

Curt flies back down to the yard and adds, "You know what? I am proud of my looks. I have earned my scruffiness by how hard I work for food!"

"I know what you mean," declares the lady. "I also know that when people see you swooping in and cawing at them, it doesn't help change their minds about you."

Curt responds, "Then what can I do? We birds understand each other. We are willing to share food in the feeders and yards. How can I get people to like me as much as they like the cardinals? They love them. It makes me sad and angry at the same time. I try so hard."

"Maybe that's it. Maybe you are so worried about what they think, and trying so hard to get them to like you, that you forget who you really are, a generous crow who cares."

Curt thinks about this message and responds, "Then how can I at least convince them that I am important and worthy, too?"

Lady Lily asks for time to think about it and adds, "Let's just enjoy our meal together. You see, Curt, right now you are safe. Right now you have food. Check out the blue sky that we can be a part of whenever we fly! Right now is a good moment."

"Yes, it is," agrees Curt. They eat for a few minutes in silence as both try to think of ways to make things better. Curt breaks the silence.

"I do not know how to change anyone else, especially people. They already have their minds made up about me. I know that if they had their way, I would never eat in their yards or feeders at all." They just want the bluebirds, cardinals, doves and egrets, you know, all the pretty birds."

"They don't like the squirrels, either, so you are in good company," notes Egret.

Crow chuckles, "I know; our feeder has a big old bell on it, and the squirrels can't get around it to feed in the feeder. You should see them try; it is pretty funny. I will say they are persistent."

"Yes, that is true; it is a great quality that squirrels have. They are creative, too and will try anything to get to where they want to be," Lady Lily observes. "Sometimes, sadly enough, they are hurt, too." They both drop their heads in sadness for that thought.

Curt shares, "I am glad that I can eat at the feeders. Sometimes I push the food off so that others can have some. The squirrels seem to like it when I do this."

Lady Lily chimes in, "I am sure they appreciate that. You know what is funny, Curt? As much as the people admire me, I can't get to the feeders. They are too high for us, and we certainly cannot perch on the edges." They both laugh at that image. Lady Lily continues, "but there is enough food in the ground and in the pond for all of us, especially if you like lizards, fish, and worms." Curt crinkles his eyes and cringes at the thought of going fishing. They both laugh.

"You know," Curt declares, "there is always enough food for all of us. When I don't see any food right away or if there is no feeder, I look deeper and use my beak to find grubs." He thinks for a moment and laughs. "I did this one day, and one of the people came out of her house chasing me with flapping arms. I thought she might actually fly away herself. What would surprise her is that I was actually helping her save her lawn as I ate."

"It is ironic," Lady Lily comments, "that sometimes those that help the most are chased away and misunderstood by the very people benefitting from their service."

"But she didn't even give me a chance!" Curt grew a little huffy. "Her loss. The grubs took over her lawn."

Lady Lily remarks, "You didn't need those grubs anyway." They laugh.

"They were good, though," Curt reminisces.

Lady Lily continues their conversation, "You know, Curt, I was just thinking about something you said about all of us liking different things. You are so right; Cardinals love the sunflower seeds. Heron and Anhinga love the fish in the pond. Finches like thistle, and hummingbirds like the nectar from flowers. I personally enjoy the sport of hunting those lizards and fish. You like digging in the ground for grubs and are satisfied with feeders and yard food."

"That is true, and because we like different things, we have plenty," Curt observes. "If all of us liked the same thing, we could run out, and we wouldn't get along as well because we would all be after the same thing. I cannot imagine trying to get the liquid out of the hummingbird's feeder."

"Nor can I," laughs Lady Lily. "Those holes are so tiny." They both chuckle at the thought of both birds with larger beaks trying to get nectar out of the tiny feeders.

Curt confides, "I think I like being different; I don't have to be like you, even though you are tall and beautiful. I used to be jealous of the cardinals, but I feel better now just knowing we are different, and that is good. I like a more of a variety of food than they do, anyway."

Lady Lily pauses. "Our creator did a great job of planning all of that. Everything works out when we accept each other and our differences and are able to share time, food, and space. If only the people understood that, they would be happier and not worry so much, and they would get along a lot better. I wish there was something we could do to help them be more content and accept all of us."

Curt wonders for a moment and exclaims, "How can we help them? We're birds! They're people! We don't even speak the same language!"

Lady Lily looks at the people in the window and thinks about Curt's question. She notices that the people are looking through the window at the two birds. "We may be starting this moment with you and me talking and eating our bounty together right in front of them. We are setting an example. The first and most important step to helping others learn is to practice what we want to teach!"

Crow exclaims, "Yes, we are setting a fine example. Good point! I am so excited! We have begun to help!"

"Curt, always know that you are a handsome incredible bird. You keep trying no matter what, and you care. In that body is a tough old bird with a big heart."

"Lady Lily, you are a wise and stunning bird. Thank you for helping me today. You turned my day from an angry one into a special one."

"And thank you for sharing our meal while helping others get along like we do. Isn't that what life is all about anyway, helping to make life better for everyone we meet no matter what?"

"I love that thought, Lady Lily. Thank you. We all have a reason to be here, and it is all about helping. You helped me, and I am grateful."

From inside the house, there is a burst of laughter.

"Look at those two birds out there! The tall and the short; the magnificent with the scrappy."

"If I didn't know better, I would think they were conversing like we are."

"And sharing a meal, too."

"I don't think I have ever seen two more unlikely companions! How funny!"

Just then, the television newscaster announces another act of violence. The people in the house shake their heads and frown in sadness.

The owner of the house looks outside, pauses, and says, "Those two birds seem happy. They are so different, but they share the yard in peace. Wouldn't it be great if the whole world was like those two birds?"

Lady Lily Egret and Curt the Crow smile at each other. Lady Lily whispers, "See, we got them thinking and talking about us and how well we get along."

"Look! They're taking our picture!"

Lady Lily smiles, "Yes, and they will remember this day and share our friendship with their friends. They will also think of you fondly."

"Lady Lily, did we just make a difference?"

"Yes, Curt, we did."

# The Weepy Willow's
## CHILDREN

Jesus said, "Let the little children come to me, and do not hinder them, for the kingdom of heaven belongs to such as these." -Matthew 19:14 NIV

In the deep corner of the backyard behind the swing set, sits a lone weeping willow. Her branches are thick with drooping leaves that swing down to the ground. There she hangs in great beauty, but no one notices her.

She knows of her perfection, but it does not do any good. No one tends to her. She is fortunate to live far in the back on the banks of a quiet pond, so her continual thirst is always quenched.

Sometimes she feels useful when the birds temporarily perch on her branches, or beautiful butterflies dance in circles between her leaves and all around, but that is only a temporary feeling.

She knows she has a purpose, but she does not know what it is. What can she do? She lives each day in a yearning contentment, wanting to be more useful while she enjoys the pleasures of just living. Somehow, even though comfortable, she feels that life goes on around her as it passes her by.

As usual, children run freely through the yard and play on their swing set. There Willow sits, watching the children with curiosity as they play imaginative games in the yard.

She worries when the children venture near because they might pull on her branches. She does not encourage them to stay. She fears their youthful abandon as she watches them playing happily on the swings.

Willow weeps. In her weeping, her branches grow closer to the ground, protecting her trunk and inner self from outside potential harms. She becomes more and more locked into herself and more fearful of the children.

She awakens the next morning asking God to help her find something that she can do that is more long lasting than providing a temporary play place for birds and butterflies.

God answers with something she did not expect to hear. "You are meant to be a safe place for all creatures to play, rest, and be safe. You are special; be patient and fear not; your prayers are answered."

She waits for a long time, wondering when her prayer will be answered. God reminds her that it already is answered and she must be patient. Occasionally, a bird, butterfly, or even a squirrel visits her, but this is no different than before her prayer. Nothing new ever happens. She begins to question her experience with God. What if what she thought was God's answer was all in her imagination? She silences that thought, and tries to stay patient and positive as God directs, but it is so hard.

One morning, she hears the children playing. She tenses up, but then remembers that God told her to be brave, so she takes a deep breath and relaxes. "I will trust," she reassures herself.

"What do you want to do?" Asks Anne.

"I want to play house," replies Gracie.

Anne reminds Gracie, "We do not have a playhouse. We need to ask Mom for one so we can play house."

Gracie looks around the yard. "We can make a little house under the slide on the swing set." They both agree to do this, but the space is very small indeed. They agree that there was only space for one in that house. Their house needs room for more people.

Willow thinks that her beautiful branches would make a fine gentle playhouse for the children. She also knows that the game of House will not hurt her. She tosses her branches in the breeze to get the girls' attention.

Anne notices and remarks, "Hey, I have an idea. Look at the Weeping Willow in the corner. I never really noticed her before, but she would make a great playhouse! Let's go see!"

The two girls venture to the back corner of the yard, and gently separate the curtain of branches. "This is a fine house," said Gracie.

The girls bring their dolls, trinkets, and plastic dinner set to an area under the tree. They lay towels to carpet their new home and set up house. Throughout the day, they enjoy a picnic, imagination games, and their dolls take those important naps while they read their books.

They play there for hours. Willow feels useful and at peace. The children's voices and joy bring her great songs of life and happiness. She loves this and realizes that this was what she is created to do.

She breathes deeply as to provide clean air for the children. They enjoy the freshness of their new location. She sings with the wind as her leaves tossed the air, and the children sing, make up stories, and read in their new house.

At lunchtime, their mother calls them in, and she sees them emerging from the tree. "What were you all playing today?" She asks.

"We were playing house," replies Anne.

Their mother asks, "Oh, would you like a play house?"

Willow hears the question and cringes with worry and fear. "Oh no, what if they want to have a perfect little playhouse? Then they would never want to play under my branches again." She grows weepy with sad thoughts thinking how and why anyone who could have a playhouse would ever venture under her branches again.

It does not occur to her that the children love her hospitality that they cannot think of a better place to be. Gracie is quick to answer her mother, "No, Mom. Willow is the perfect playhouse. We can pretend and make it anything we want."

Anne adds, "Her walls are the best! We can walk through them or stay inside! We have light from the sun, but most of all, Willow sings to us. A house made of dead wood cannot do that."

Willow hears this, smiles a teary smile of love, and breathes a sigh of relief. Her newfound peace is real, and all is well. She is needed and loved. This thought carries her through the rainy days when there are no visitors and also through the times when the children are in school.

Their playhouse changes as the children do. Instead of the towels and children's chairs, there are small benches and a table set under her branches.

As they grow, the children still seek her peaceful solitude. They take their studies and reading out under her branches, and she helps them learn. They have fresh air and can think clearly. Anne and Gracie are good students who love studying under Willow's guidance, where they can concentrate, and their imaginations expand.

As they reach their teen years, friends join them under the branches, where they set up their tables with all sorts of refreshments. Sometimes, there are games like croquet or even bocce ball. Other times, they sit and chat about their interests, dreams, and lives.

Willow cherishes these times, and she becomes an important part of the girls' lives, and they become the central part in hers. Willow grows tall, thick, and content.

Then suddenly, the girls' visits stop. Willow does not know what is happening. She questions herself, "Did I do something wrong? Why did the girls just go away without saying goodbye?"

Months go by, and one weary afternoon, Anne visits alone. Willow is so happy to see her, but something is wrong. Anne is on the bench crying. Willow sends her a branch for comfort, and Anne holds it tightly to her chest. Anne takes a deep breath, thanks Willow, and tells her she will be okay. She is returning to college and will always be sad about the loss of one of the high school friends who had spent time with them under the tree. Willow is saddened with this news and comforts her. She also wonders where Gracie is. Gracie is always there for Anne.

As if understanding, Anne tells Willow that Gracie has exams and cannot leave college. "I so miss her being here with me, but I'm happy you are here, Willow."

Anne slowly walks back to the house, and Willow is alone again. The birds and butterflies keep her company, but she misses her children.

A few weeks later, one bright shiny morning, Willow awakens to a great surprise. Anne and Gracie approach, gently separate her branches, and sit on the bench under her canopy. They chat about their future plans. "You know what, Anne?" Gracie announces. "This is the perfect place, right here under our dear Willow.

"Yes, Gracie, it is. Thank you, Willow! We love you! This is the perfect place." Willow rustles her leaves and sends her branches to each girl to hug them as she wonders, "the perfect place for what?"

It does not take long for her to receive an answer. One day, there were many rows of chairs in the backyard.  At the end of each row was a flower arrangement. A white carpet led from Willow, down the middle aisle, to a gazebo with flowing vines and flowers.

A beaming bride and her maid of honor sneak under Willow's branches and prepare for their entrance. A harp plays as the birds sing. Willow's branches harmonize along with them.

"Gracie, you are a beautiful bride!" exclaims Anne. "And this is the perfect place, in our playhouse under the Willow with our backyard playground hosting all the best days of our lives, including this one."

"Yes, Anne. We set up our first house here as children. We pretended how we would be when we were grown up, and now here we are. I always felt that the Willow's home was holy ground, where our spirits and imaginations soared. It was here that we felt her love and nurturing. So my dear sister, I now begin a new chapter in my life with another in this perfect place where it all began, the place where we imagined life would be perfect, and it is.

Willow beams, and her branches softly brush the bride and her sister as if trying to hug them. The girls hold the branches and each other. Anne asks the tree for forgiveness as she clips a small tip off of one of her branches. Willow is shocked; the girls had never hurt her before, but then she smiles as Anne puts the tip into Gracie's beautiful bridal bouquet, making it more magnificent.

Willow is bursting with joy, and the sting did not last long. She loves Anne and Grace and sways in harmony with the harp as part of her branch walks down the aisle with the beaming bride and is with her when she takes her vows.

The wedding is splendid. Afterward, the bride and groom stand together at the willow for their pictures. One of the pictures captures Willow's gentle touching embrace of the newlyweds. All the people enjoy the special peaceful setting, and Willow stands tall, providing grand shade when anyone needs it.

Before the bride throws her bouquet, she removes the branch and key flowers to save in her bridal book. A little piece of the willow will be with her forever.

Willow feels fulfilled knowing she plays an important role in making life better for Anne and Grace, just as they do for her.

There is a day just a few years later when children burst through the back door and play house under her branches.

Willow continues to grow tall, full, and wise into her old age and thinks back to her weepy worries from long ago. "I do not know why I worried so much. My prayers were answered far and beyond my worries and dreams. I am forever thankful for this amazing life filled with love and laughter. My purpose may be humble, and that's perfect for me. "Thank you, God," she prayed, "for my backyard family. They have brought love and joy to my life, and I am blessed."

This is where we end these sweet snippets of love and life in our magical backyard garden.

May all of us find special peace in creation and with each other, and I hope these little stories brighten your days and fill them with sweet blessings.

I end with a prayer for our common journey:

I pray that every day, we find our peaceful place, grow in gratitude for this amazing universe, and share love, laughter, and life with all creation. When we do this, we are all one.

God bless you, and may you enjoy abundant blessings of peace, joy, and love in this incredible journey of life.

# Appendix

All of my little stories are written with the intention of helping all who read them find peace, joy, and love in the world.

This book is written for all ages, for the themes are applicable to all. It can also serve as a conversation and conservation starter. Because I cannot get the inborn educator out of my system, I am providing adults some ideas they can do with their children or each other as they explore nature in our parks, in their travels, or in their own neighborhoods and backyards. In the notes, I list the characters with the invitation to notice them when you see them in the world and thank them for being with us.

The most blessed gift we can give our children is the time spent reading to them every day, even if is only a few minutes spent in a short story. In rearing our child, bedtime is the perfect time to clean up the day's mess, read together, and pray together. As we read and lead with our fingers under the words, before long, our child understands the concept of reading and learning to read. Soon the lines of letters blend into sentences, paragraphs, and thoughts.

We also find that children understand whatever words parents teach them. It doesn't matter if you begin with one or three syllable words, your children will understand what you teach, so using larger words with the smaller words increases vocabulary and comprehension skills.

My little stories are created to help children (and adults) experience the beauty around them, understand some of nature's magnificent workings, and have a respect for our earth. Also, it is my hope that they learn to feel blessed by simple times spent alone and with family. I do not talk down to them. If they are too young to read these independently, then I invite parents to read with them and share thoughts and meaning as they read. Quiet time with children becomes a special gift no one can ever remove.

When our children hear these stories being read, and as they learn to read these books for themselves, they learn the joyful life lessons of finding peace and love within our world and without having to venture farther than the backyard or kitchen windows.

Let's make this world a better place for all, including our children, by helping them absorb simple goodness and God-ness that is within and surrounding all of this divine and glorious creation we call life.

For this purpose, I created a resource for discussion, recording experiences, and ideas for sharing. I invite all to take a journey to the backyard, a local park, the beach, or in your neighborhoods. Celebrate all you see, talk about our amazing lives with others, and add your own stories to this little book.

| From the story "The Spirit of the Tree" | Things to talk about | Child's comments, insights, or drawings |
|---|---|---|
| "I think that I shall never see<br><br>A poem as lovely as a tree"<br><br>Joyce Kilmer | Trees are pretty, and all are different. Have your child look at some of the trees outside your window and ask what is pretty or different about it. Even if it is winter, and there are no leaves, the shape of even one branch might be unusual enough to talk about. | |

| From the story "The Spirit of the Tree" | Things to talk about | Child's comments, insights, or drawings |
|---|---|---|
| The birds nested in her branches, and the herons shared perch time at her peak with the anhingas, kingfishers, and egrets as they watched the lake below for the fish that would become their meal. | See the bird list and identify the birds in your backyards. Are any the same as the ones in the story? | |

| From the story "The Spirit of the Tree" | Things to talk about | Child's comments, insights, or drawings |
|---|---|---|
| Cardinals danced gracefully around her peak, and landed softly on her branches. A tiny sparrow sat in the feeder hanging from the lowest branch. Mama Blue Jay tossed food from the feeder onto the ground where the babies were eating. | Look at the birds outside. Watch them and talk about each one. Name them or make up stories about them. | |
| Squirrels playfully chased each other up and down her trunk. | Are there squirrels in your yard, or have you seen them on walks? Are they playing, running, jumping, or eating. | |

| From the story "The Spirit of the Tree" | Things to talk about | Child's comments, insights, or drawings |
|---|---|---|
| The rabbit ate at the rye grass growing between the knees. | Did you know rabbits are in the wild? Not all bunnies have long ears. Small brown rabbits with short ears, are called "Swamp Rabbits." | |
| She took a deep breath, and filled her being with carbon dioxide. She exhaled the oxygen for the people and animals to breathe. It was the cleanest of air and didn't need any filtering or perfumes. It provided the essence of life for so many. | Even the act of breathing is a miracle. What children may not know is trees breathe in what we breathe out, and we breathe in what trees breathe out. | |

| From the story "The Spirit of the Tree" | Things to talk about | Child's comments, insights, or drawings |
|---|---|---|
| In this great big world, one tree could help so many. | Every tree, just like every person and every part of creation counts and has purpose. | |
| She may not have been one who could run and play, but that was not her job. Her job was to be there and help those around her. | We each have a purpose for every moment we spend on earth. Sometimes the purpose is to give hugs; other times it is to teach, learn, or help others. What are ways we can help others and our world? | |

| From the story "The Spirit of the Tree" | Things to talk about | Child's comments, insights, or drawings |
|---|---|---|
| She too marveled at the creation. She watched the baby finches, the cardinal family, the sparrows, jays, and crows enjoy the beautiful trees. She looked at the majestic one and discerned a special spirit about it. It seemed to have a halo that was filled with love and comfort. | Think for a few minutes on the beauty of creation and how precious each life is. | |

| From the story "The Spirit of the Tree" | Things to talk about | Child's comments, insights, or drawings |
|---|---|---|
| So the little girl went to the tree and put her hand on it, feeling the pulse of life and energy. | Stop and feel the trees, smell the flowers, and feel the love in nature. | |
| The girl marveled at how amazing the creation of the tree was.<br><br>The tree marveled at how amazing the creation of the girl was. | Note that all are divine creations. Look at each spec of nature. Find the beauty in each. | |

| From the story "The Spirit of the Tree" | Things to talk about | Child's comments, insights, or drawings |
|---|---|---|
| What they did not know was this moment was being shared by many children and grown ups all over the world at the exact same time. Some were gazing at stars, others at the ocean, and some from the mountains. You see, the spirit of life's energy is everywhere. When everyone is feeling this love and peace at the same time, only love and peace can happen where they are. | Share this moment with another. See if they were enjoying the beauty of the moment, too. Share what you saw, felt, heard, and noticed. | |

| From the story "The Spirit of the Tree" | Things to talk about | Child's comments, insights, or drawings |
|---|---|---|
| The girl says a little prayer:<br><br>Thank you dear Creator for this beautiful earth.<br><br>Thank you for the tree and all it does for the animals and me.<br><br>Thank you for all life.<br><br>Thank you for showing me the divine miracle that all creation is. | Say a prayer of thanks for this precious time, place, and creation. | |

| From the story "The Spirit of the Tree" | Things to talk about | Child's comments, insights, or drawings |
|---|---|---|
| I have to go now, so help me remember this all the time, even when times are hard, or the world seems mean. The world is not mean here; it is sweet and good. Thank you for keeping this in my mind, my heart, and my spirit. | | |

| From the story "The Spirit of the Tree" | Things to talk about | Child's comments, insights, or drawings |
|---|---|---|
| The world became a better place.<br><br>Just like her backyard.<br><br>And the tree grew in love, knowing that this love, when spread, saves the world.<br><br>If each one of us takes a little joy and love and spreads it around, love, peace, and joy will overcome everything else. | Note how the world is getting better when people love, smile, and are at peace with each other. | |

| From the story "The Spirit of the Tree" | Things to talk about | Child's comments, insights, or drawings |
|---|---|---|
| Your insights and ideas | | |
| | | |

**"The Window"** is a very special story about a girl and her grandmother. Record special times spent with grandparents and relatives, especially if they are sharing something they love. Go back and re-read these from time to time. As children spend time with their relatives, have them write these down or draw a picture and put them in this book.

| When and ages | What did your loved ones share with you? | Draw pictures or describe your feelings and details |
|---|---|---|
|  |  |  |
|  |  |  |
|  |  |  |
|  |  |  |

Also, in "The Window," at the end we see the grown girl, now a mother and her daughter carrying on in the same way. Every act of sweet peace and love that is passed from one to another continues from heart to heart, spirit to spirit, and forever connects all of us to those who lived before and those who will live in generations to come. What sweet family traditions and practices from the past will you share with those in the future? List them here and tell where they came from (as far as you know).

_____

_____

_____

In **"The River Tree"'s Story,"** the children enjoy and honor their world and the shape of the tree. What can children and all of us do to honor our world and the various "shapes" within each part of creation? Look at the story of how and why the tree is twisted and shaped for good. It was scary at first for the tree, but then she used her new shape to help. Is the same true with people? As you explore, try to find trees that have unusual shapes; take their pictures and make up stories about them. Add them to this page.

In "**The Forgotten Garden,**" two sisters share time together cleaning out clutter from the back of the house their parents shared. Talk about your house and picture it in 20, 30, or 40 years. What would your children find?

Create your own special garden. Together, find a lovely planter, large or small, and create a succulent and cactus garden. Find a special place for it and care for it together. Take a picture of it and place it here.

**"The Lady Lily and Curt the Crow"** is about getting along with those who are different and setting examples of the behaviors we expect from others, even when we have been wronged. When you or your children see others being treated without respect (even if they are wrong), what is the best way to respond? What examples can you and your children set for others? Begin to live this example with them. Write some of them down, and when someone takes your picture doing this, record it in this book and see if you can get a copy of this picture to add to the story.

_____

_____

_____

_____

_____

_____

_____

_____

**"The Weepy Willow's Children"** is about life, contentment and the purpose. Find a place (preferably outside – not one behind closed doors unless nothing else is available) for each family member to find peace, solitude, and privacy for imaginative play or reflection. Record which place each person chooses and why. Save these little notes for later; as each person ages or grows up, what types of places to they choose for renewal, peace, and solitude. Are they similar or different? Are they visited often throughout life? Record them here:

_____

_____

_____

_____

_____

_____

_____

Notes – Cast of Characters – Find them in the world and write down where they are and what they are doing.

| Character | Where/When | What were they doing? |
|---|---|---|
| Anhinga | | |
| Bird feeders/bird baths | | |
| Blue Jay | | |
| Butterflies | | |
| Mr. and Madame Cardinal | | |
| Curt the Crow | | |
| Cypress Tree | | |
| Ducks | | |
| Lady Lily Egret | | |
| Finches | | |
| Glossy Ibis | | |
| Golden Ball Cactus | | |
| Gary Grackle | | |
| Herons | | |
| Kingfishers | | |
| Moorhens | | |
| Mourning Doves of Peace | | |
| Mrs. Quail | | |
| Rabbits | | |

| Character | Where/When | What were they doing? |
| --- | --- | --- |
| Rainbows | | |
| Red-winged blackbirds | | |
| Riverbanks (note the unusual trees, too) | | |
| Robin Redbreast | | |
| Sweet Sparrows | | |
| Squirrels | | |
| Stars | | |
| Sun | | |
| Twisted Tree | | |
| Weeping Willow | | |
| Young child(ren) playing trees | | |
| Youth fishing | | |
| Others | | |

# Bibliography of Quotations

Alexander, Cecil Frances. "All Things Bright and Beautiful." *Hymns for Little Children. 1848*

"The Wizard of Oz (1939)." Goodreads, Film, www.goodreads.com/work/quotes/1993810-the-wonderful-wizard-of-oz.

Hine, Stuart K. "How Great Thou Art." *Lift Every Voice and Sing II. Church Publishing Incorporated, NY 1993:60.*

Kilmer, Joyce. "Trees." *The Best Loved Poems of the American People.* Doubleday NY 1936: 561.

Miles, Austin. In the Garden." *Lift Every Voice and Sing II.* Church Publishing Incorporated, NY 1993:69.

Unknown composer or lyricist. Slave Songs aka African American Spirituals. "Down to the River to Pray." 1861-1865. Hymns.me.uk.

Additional Notes and Memories:

# About the Author

Nancy Nason Guss is a retired educator of 37 years. Prior to retiring, she was a principal at two education centers for five and a half years, an assistant principal at a middle and high school for 11 and a half years, and a middle school language arts teacher for 20 years. She holds a Master's of Education degree in Educational Leadership and a Bachelor of Arts degree in Speech Communication/English Education, both from the University of South Florida, Tampa.

Nancy begins each day in meditation and prayer surrounded by the life within her garden and in her backyard. The playful antics and visits from the beautiful birds and critters have inspired these stories, as have memories and experiences from her childhood and travels.

She tries to find, celebrate, honor, and recognize each person and our earth as divine creations and gifts from God, and hopes to bring that deep down contented joy, peace, and love to all through remembering all the simple blessings and pleasures we enjoy together on this planet that we all share.

Printed in the United States
By Bookmasters